AF207700

WARMEST
WISHES!
Shelley Kaplan
&
Robert W. Hutchison

Highland School Library
Sudman Valley

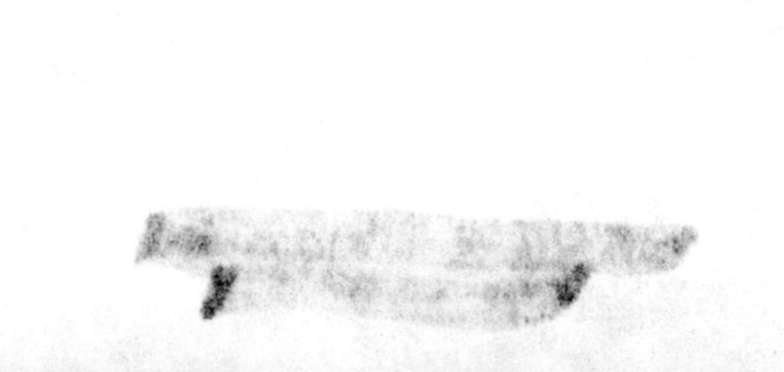

SONGS FOR SCRATCHING MOSQUITO BITES AND PETTING THE CAT

by
Shelley Kaplan

illustrated by
Robert W. Hutchison

SONGS FOR SCRATCHING MOSQUITO BITES
AND
PETTING THE CAT

by
Shelley Kaplan

illustrated by
Robert W. Hutchison

10 9 8 7 6 5 4 3 2 1
FIRST EDITION

TEXT COPYRIGHT © 1997 by Shelley Kaplan
ILLUSTRATION COPYRIGHT © 1997 by Robert W. Hutchison

LIBRARY OF CONGRESS CATALOG CARD NUMBER: 97-94201
ISBN: 0-9631833-1-1

ALSO AVAILABLE FROM KAPLAN PRESS:

CHAMELEON
by
Shelley Kaplan
ISBN: 0-9631833-0-3

ALL RIGHTS RESERVED. NO PART OF THIS BOOK MAY BE REPRODUCED OR TRANSMITTED IN ANY FORM OR BY ANY MEANS, ELECTRONIC OR MECHANICAL, INCLUDING PHOTOCOPYING, RECORDING, OR BY ANY INFORMATION STORAGE AND RETRIEVAL SYSTEM WITHOUT WRITTEN PERMISSION FROM THE PUBLISHER, EXCEPT FOR THE INCLUSION OF BRIEF QUOTATIONS IN A REVIEW.

FOR INFORMATION ADDRESS:

KAPLAN PRESS   P.O. BOX 6148   CHICAGO, IL 60680-6148

Typeset by Carol Backe Creative, Forest Park, IL 60130

Printed in the United States of America

Highland School Library
Stillman Valley

For Robert, my heart, who saw my voice.

For my parents, Rose and Jack, who read to me.

For my sister, Ilene, my first listening partner.

—S.K.

For Shelley, who gave me the love, the inspiration, and the opportunity.

For my parents, Clyde and Jane.

For the children who will look with new eyes at what I have drawn.

—R.W.H.

MOTHER OF PEARL

Has anyone seen the mother of Pearl?

Early this morning
    she lost her,
    when out of her cloister
    the poor Mrs. Oyster
        fell to the ocean
            which tossed her
            into the foam
                and up on the waves—

Is this the way that a mother behaves?!!

Don't cry, little girl,
    for the mother of Pearl
        will return with the waves
        to the shore.

She'll bring you a ring,
    and she'll promise to cling
        to her shell
            and to latch up her door.

GRASSHOPPER

A grasshopper dressed in best grasshopper green
is a fellow who rarely, if ever, is seen
as long as he hides in the grass and the weeds
and none of his neighbors pauses and reads
the sign that politely states:

KEEP OFF THE GRASS
(no one permitted a grasshopper pass)

Then the poor fellows must all hop away,
looking for places to live and to play
where grown-ups don't bother complaining with signs
and children enjoy making grass stain designs.

HOPPING MAD
LEAVES OF GRASS
LEAVING TOWN
LEAPS OF FAITH
YARD SOODS

FLY

If I were a fly
    I would try to defy
the evil-eyed hand
    of a swatter.

I'd buzz and I'd swoop
    and I'd fly loop-de-loop,
and no one would cry out,
    "I got her!"

ANT

Ant can't wait to picnic.
At table she is rude.
She calls her friends to dine with her.
  Then runs across the food!

And she prefers to eat the sweetest treat
  that she can find,
 while passing up the vegetables
  and those who run behind!

MOSQUITO

Does mosquito itch inside herself
  before she bites my leg?

Does she lay her itches on my skin
  like chicken lays her egg?

I've seen the pink nest that she leaves
  to roost upon my skin.

How come itches don't fall out
  the way that they fell in?

BAT

The bat in upstairs attic,
   when hanging from his toes,
 leads a topsy-turvy life,
   as everybody knows!

His top hat is his bottom.
   His smile is a frown.
The floor, for bat, is ceiling.
   His world is upside-down.

But he doesn't need a night-light.
   The dark, he never fears.
At that, the bat won't bat an eye.
   He sees us with his ears.

Three cheers for bat, that battered beast,
   whose praise is seldom heard.
But, when we cheer, how will he hear?
   How will he get the word?

DUCKS

"Eat your sandwich. Eat the spread.
Eat the filling. Eat your bread."

I eat it all,
   except, I dread to eat the crust.
      Of it, I am not fond.
      But, I have found a trick!
         I bring it to the pond.
         And there, I throw it to the ducks!
         Yoo-hoo! Look out below.
         The ducks must eat my crust, ho-ho!

         Every puddle's a street
            for the waterproof feet of the duck.
         What a lucky-go-happy!

         Slapping his toes,
            there he goes through the pond.

         And it suits him
            to see me
            in my yellow slicker.

         He snickers and quacks
            while he waddles away
            as I pull on my boots
            before I can play.

CRUSTACEA

PEACOCK

How entrancing is the dancing of the proudly fancy
peacock!
No matter what the weather.
Each feather firmly tethered to his bottom.

And in autumn, when he struts about the yard,
a bard would find it hard to do him justice
for his beauty!

When he spreads his fanny
—Can he?—
Yes, he can!
And what a fanfare!
He can fan himself in sunshine.
In the rain, it's his umbrella.

What a fellow is the peacock,
with his finely feathered fan!

And I, too, proudly wave my fluffy fan
when I am hot.
It is grand to hold it in my hand.
The finest, fancy fan I own, imported from Japan.

ELEPHANT

With the fingers in his nose,
an elephant can seize
the tiniest of peanuts
and pick it up, with ease!

But where does peanut go?
Does it make one toenail grow?

"Oh, no!"
the elephant replies.
"It is to him, I owe my size!"

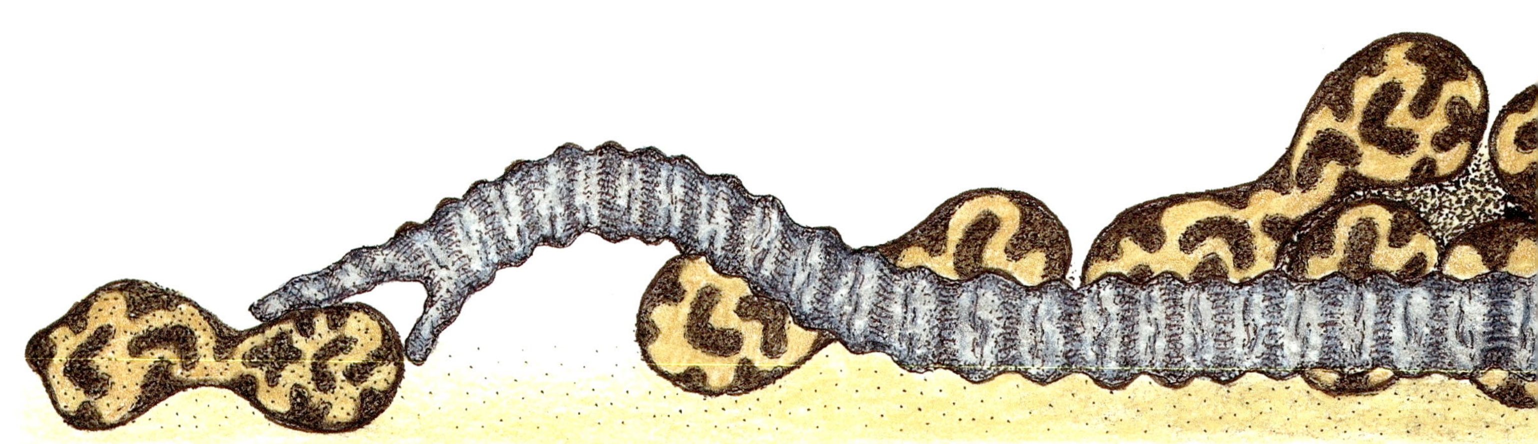

SNAKE

Who could find a bigger pig than snake?
He eats until he breaks.

First, the head peels off,
and then,
the tail.
A trail of skin
is left behind.

Unveiled,
the snake beneath
reminds us of
the first—
the one before
he burst!

As for me,
I know that as I grow
I'll change my shape,
my size,
my style.
But I wouldn't for the world
trade my smile—
or my skin.
I'm happy that my outside grows as quickly as my in!

CAT

The cat's pink tongue
   licks her bowl
      before she rolls it
   through her fur,
      purring as she licks it clean.
Preening, for a cat, is tasty
   if she's fed on fattening pastry.

I, too, lick my fingers
   one by one.
It's fun to lick
   until the grown-ups frown:

   "Use some water."
   "Use some soap."

   Someday,
      I'll be a cat,
      I hope!

MILK

CAMEL

A desert ship is camel:

In stately caravan,
    the waves of saddled
      humped-backs
    float across the sand.

Atop the crest, a treasure.
Beneath, the undertow:
    the precious store of
      water
    enabling the flow.

OCTOPUS

Bedecked, inside his vessel, in his gallant coat-of-arms,
the octopus, in daydreams, displays his knightly charms.

He's the handiest of fellows. There is nothing he can't do.
As a one-man armed armada, he's both skipper and the crew.

He can handle every crisis. Keep a finger in each pot.
But on one hand, though he's ready, on the other, he is not.

He could sail away to anywhere. He harbors thoughts of Rome,
while drifting through the hours as he sits in port, at home.

Bedecked, inside his vessel, in his gallant coat-of-arms,
the octopus, in daydreams, displays his knightly charms

while anchored to his armchair
where he rests his weary limbs,

drowning in the groundswell
of his thoughts, as daylight dims.

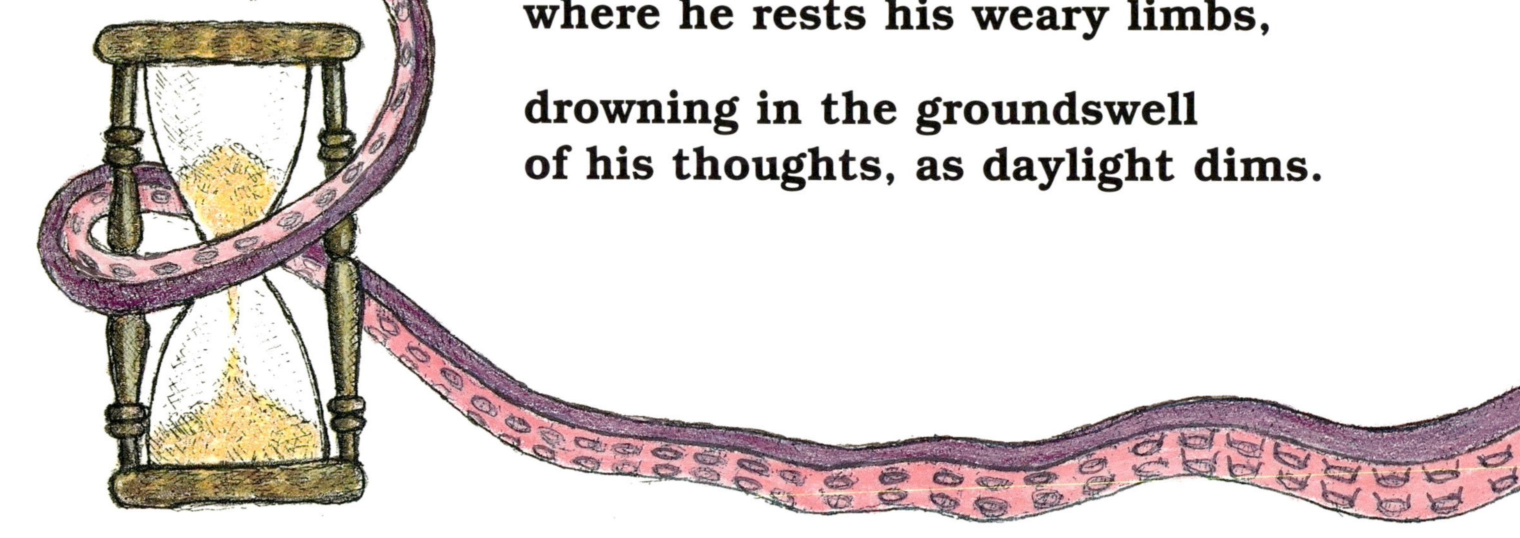

ROME
PORT AU PRINCE

THE VOICE OF THE TURTLE

Inside my shell,
I'm well,
myself!
And everything
upon my shelf!

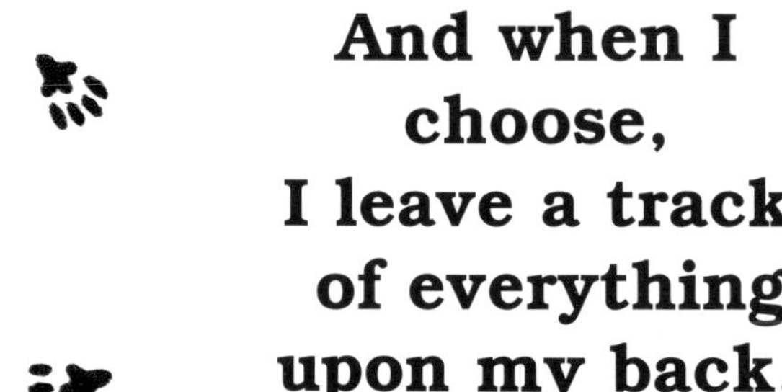

And when I
choose,
I leave a track
of everything
upon my back.

My footprints
on the
path repeat
the story
that is
in my
feet.

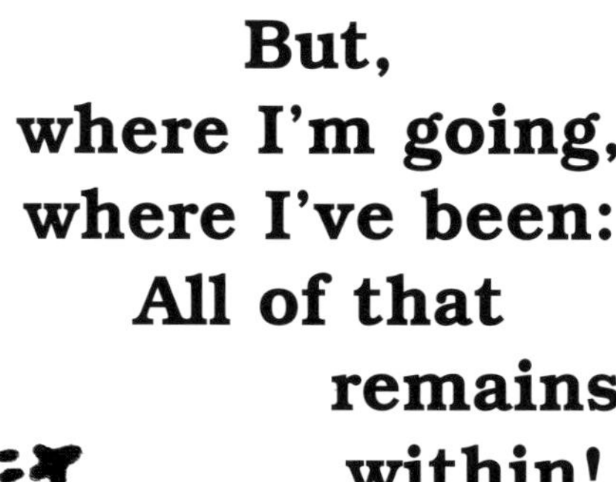

But,
where I'm going,
where I've been:
All of that
remains
within!

Not too big
and not too small,
not too wide
and not too tall:

—My house—
The perfect size for
ME
and I, alone, possess
the key!